D1572457

Is **Change**
Making
Your
Career a
Three-Ring
Circus?

RINGMASTER

8 Strategies for Becoming a
★ ★ ★ **Star Performer** ★ ★ ★
in the Midst of Change

David W. Hults

CEO of Activ:8 Careers
Author of
From Cornered To Corner Office

W.L.
Nelson
PRESS

RINGMASTER:
8 STRATEGIES FOR BECOMING A STAR PERFORMER IN THE MIDST OF CHANGE

BY DAVID W. HULTS, FOUNDER AND CEO OF ACTIV:8 CAREERS

PUBLISHED BY W.L. NELSON PRESS
ST. LOUIS, MISSOURI

PRINTED IN USA

ISBN-13 978-0-9790494-1-5
ISBN-10 0-9790494-1-5

8-30-13

Gladys,

What a true
friend you are.
Thank you for your
support over the years."

Best of Success,

David DeSheus

RINGMASTER

★ ★ ★ ★ ★ ★

by DAVID W. HULTS

Table Of Contents

RINGMASTER

Introduction

by JUDY NELSON
Former Senior Organizational Development HR Professional,
Express Scripts

David and I had lunch the day after I previewed this book. I was excited to tell him how much I loved it. I was able to really visualize the points he was making, and as a result, I could easily learn and remember them. There were so many ideas that could help anyone wanting to understand change.

However, I had one fear. His writing on the subject of managing career change was so simple to "get" that I was afraid people would skim it for ideas, ultimately not doing the work necessary to learn what he was saying.

As I was telling David about my fear over lunch, he interrupted me and asked if I would write this introduction – to help make sure YOU get the most out of this book. And that's something I intend to do.

Don't just simply glide through *Ringmaster*, reading page after page, thinking to yourself, "This is great stuff. What a unique way of looking at change." Thinking it's good advice isn't enough. You need to **do the work** if you want to gain real understanding of yourself and how you can better manage change – and how to use that knowledge in today's business world.

I've read many business books that cover the same career-oriented topics over and over. But, I have yet to read one that has such a helpful section on interviewing for a promotion, and that's saying something. Reading it, you know David's been there. The insights he offers are invaluable.

Do NOT skip the exercises! They are there for a reason, one building on the last and preparing for the next. Do the work this book outlines! It will ultimately pay you enormous dividends.

And then there's the biggest "exercise" of them all – the assessment. It will provide you with a better understanding of who you really are, what you have to offer, and how to best manage yourself when faced with continual change.

Since I was given the privilege of writing this introduction, I feel obligated to close with something profound. So, here it is – a quote by Steve Jobs. The way David wrote this book brought it to mind:

"Simple can be harder than complex. You have to work hard to get your thinking clean to make it simple. But it's worth it in the end because once you get there, you can move mountains."

My hope for you is that you take this book seriously, do the work, and finally, enjoy watching what happens!

Author's Note

To live is to change. We are constantly altering, rearranging and growing in our lives, both professionally and personally. I have learned that if I can look at "forced" changes as opportunities (rather than fighting changes and seeing myself as a victim), I will take steps toward a more meaningful life.

But that's a lot easier to write about than to do.

Since I believe that we all answer to a higher power – God, the universe – I think there is a reason you have come in contact with this book. It's up to you to ask *why*. What's going on in your work and life right now that involves change? Are you prepared to manage it successfully?

Living our lives with purpose means we must go on a journey to help define what we are meant to do. And once we know our purpose, we can go about the business of fulfilling it.

The first step of that journey toward purpose and a more fulfilling life? Get comfortable with the fact that you will never really be done changing.

My hope for you is that this book will arm you with powerful change strategies that you can immediately apply to your work and your life. My clients have found that these strategies helped them transition from status quo performers to true "Ringmasters" of change – and life.

Foreword

The advertisements assured me that it would be filled with danger! And excitement! And yet, I was not fully sure what I would see when I walked into the coliseum. It quickly became clear to me that things had changed a lot over the 30 years since I had last seen the circus. Sure, the vendors still hawked cotton candy, but the souvenirs looked so different from those of my youth. Where was the monkey on a stick I remembered from so long ago? Now everything blinked, made noise, lit up or all three! As I took my seat, I heard a familiar introduction. "Welcome to *The Greatest Show On Earth®!*"

That familiar statement was one of the only things at the circus that had not changed whatsoever.

And yet, it was still the circus I had attended when I was a kid. There were marvelous acts and performances – they just weren't the same ones I had seen decades ago. The performers were still glamorous – they just seemed so much younger than the classic circus "lifers" I had seen way back when. But irrationally, I was expecting to see the same performers from 30 years ago do the same things they did 30 years ago. Sounds ridiculous, right? Then why is it that so many of us expect to do the exact same thing for 30 years in OUR careers?

Many of us want our career journey to be predictable, providing a promise of security for many years to come. I've heard so many people say to me, with surprise and sadness, "I thought I would retire doing the same thing I had been doing year after year after year. But that's all changed now."

As I sat there watching the performers wow the crowd under the lights, I couldn't help myself. I stopped watching the circus as an audience member and started viewing it as a Career Coach. I studied each of the performers, wondering what their career was like. How could these fantastic performers grow *their* careers? Where could they go from here? Is the circus exclusively a young person's game now? What happened to all the performers I saw three decades ago? Obviously they moved on to something... right? But I also noticed very specific things that served as illustrations for how to manage a great career.

For example, every performer had a unique skill set, very different from act to act. Collectively, they provided a variety of experiences around a single circus theme. One show. One purpose. As I thought about it, I realized it had some of the same building blocks organizations also use. The individual acts work together toward a greater promise to the audience – a daring and colorful experience that will amaze and entertain all ages. Every star performer supported the mission by performing outstanding acts to the best of their abilities.

But no one stood out more than the Ringmaster. He was the person in control of the show and in command of the audience's experience. He made sure that everyone was in the right place at the right time. He kept a close eye on who was performing within the three rings, even if there were three acts going on at the same time. Things were changing around him right and left, and yet he remained unfazed.

I was only seeing the magic, of course. What I didn't see were all the behind-the-scenes meetings, agreements and plans made to create and maintain a circus worthy of being called *The Greatest Show On Earth®*.

My thoughts were interrupted as I saw one of the acts almost make a potentially deadly mistake. A high-wire performer stumbled momentarily and the audience gasped, but the performer maintained balance and continued tenuously along the wire. It reminded me that even great plans and practice cannot always guarantee success. Sometimes the unexpected can change everything. If it's not a near high-wire accident, it could simply be an elephant's unexpected bathroom break (which I also had the, ahem, pleasure of experiencing!). It just goes to show that to do his job well, the Ringmaster must always be mentally prepared, expecting and embracing change.

After a few days, I thought back on my experience at the circus. Sure, there were some things I missed from my childhood. But as an adult, the changes I saw in the three circus rings had taken me to a place I couldn't have even imagined when I was a kid.

Our careers are very much like a circus in this way. If you can see change (even if it's not wanted) as an opportunity to make something you love even better, YOU can become a Ringmaster of change!

This book is not just about dealing with change, but mastering it in your career. After reading it, you should be able to answer these three questions with the confidence of a seasoned Ringmaster:

1 ▶ What are you doing to manage change in your career now and in the future?

2 ▶ Are you partnering with others to deliver change that will improve the organization?

3 ▶ How will you embrace the unexpected changes that will no doubt come?

The circus of change is about to begin.

And you're about to go from being a spectator to a star performer.

RINGMASTER

8 STRATEGIES FOR BECOMING A STAR PERFORMER IN THE MIDST OF CHANGE

★ ★ ★ ★ ★ ★

Change. It comes with the territory when you have a career. Changes to your role within an organization could come from the ever-evolving economy, new trends in your industry that impact the way business is done or any other number of things, even a promotion.

So what will you do? Will you get caught up in the chaos? Or will you be mentally prepared to shine through it and prove your value?

I want to state this warning right from the get-go: When it comes to managing your career during a time of change, the "status quo" mind-set (just taking change as it comes and rolling with the punches) will work only for a period of time. If you are not careful, you will end up in a career and have no idea how you got there!

I remember once talking with another recruiter I worked with about how exciting it was that each of us would be receiving our very own computers (this was back when computers were just being introduced into everyone's daily working life). I remember her saying to me, "I'm just scared to death of a computer!" It represented a change in the way she did her job that she was not ready for, and did not want to accept. I saw this fear in her and wanted to help. I decided to take the initiative and show her a few things on her new computer, specifically how to use the Web. I've never seen anyone learn something so fast. The very next day she came to me and said, "Did you know you can shop on the Internet?!" Her face was filled with excitement and it was clear her dread of learning a new technology was completely gone. Now, in her mind, this was the best change ever!

The point is this: People who manage their careers know how to quickly adjust and embrace change when the circus comes to town. Not every change comes with obvious positive opportunities (like being "forced" to use a new computer the way my coworker was!). You need to ask yourself what motivates you before you can focus your attention on becoming a Ringmaster of change.

8 Strategies To Become A Ringmaster

Whether you are in the driver's seat or not during an organizational change, this book will help you map out strategies for managing your career change successfully, leading to a more fulfilling career, and thereby a happier life.

We'll start by dissecting the Three Rings Of Change, followed by the 8 Strategies For Managing Change, and finish by identifying your unique Change Profile (part of this includes an interactive online assessment that's included in this book).

I've also included a "Manager's Spotlight" section at the end of each chapter. Great managers understand that their team members may each need different types of support from management to grow their careers, find new or better ways to add value or embrace and implement organizational change. The "Manager's Spotlight" will help those with direct reports and/or director-level professionals know how they can use different methods to help their teams manage change successfully.

And it all starts with the Three Rings Of Change.

RINGMASTER

The
THREE RINGS
of CHANGE

★ ★ ★ ★ ★ ★

I want you to think of all the changes you have made (or will be making) in your career and life. The fact is that you spend most of your life *not* with your closest loved ones, but working in a career that *you* decided to have. So isn't it important that your career has deeper meaning than just making money or working for retirement? That's what makes mastering change so important. To truly thrive and have meaning in your career, you need to make the most of it, and that means *making* and *managing* change, not simply reacting to it.

Your success in managing a thriving career is based on understanding three basic principles that I call the "Three Rings Of Change." And just like the three rings of a circus, the Three Rings Of Change demand simultaneous attention.

1	**2**	**3**
CENTER RING	**MIDDLE RING**	**OUTER RING**
Your **"Ring Of Control"** includes factors you can create, alter and direct to your advantage – and thereby must respond to.	Your **"Ring Of Influence"** is focused on elements upon which you can have an indirect impact through your presence and influence.	Your **"Ring Of Response"** includes all the important factors that do have an impact on your career, but that you cannot directly control or influence – and thereby must respond to.

A large part of this book is dedicated to looking at how you can create change or influence it within the context of the Three Rings Of Change. We'll look at how to respond to change that's within and outside of your control in order to manage your career in the midst of organizational shift. Naturally, let's start with Ring #1.

The Ring Of Control

We often don't recognize how much control we actually have. To prove my point, here's a very small list of the many big things we can control: attitudes, education, what we buy, whom we date or marry, where we choose to live, what we wear, our hairstyle, our eating habits, what we do with our leisure time and where we choose to put our faith. Nobody has final say in what you do with those things but YOU! But what's amazing to me is that once an individual feels their choices are limited, they draw the conclusion that they no longer have control of, or a choice about, much of anything. They have focused on the new limitations rather than the other factors they *still* control.

A friend of mine was going through a divorce and was stretched financially. He accepted a job offer he didn't really want and explained, "I didn't have a choice!" But there were reasons he was stretched financially. He believed he had to continue to live in an expensive part of town in a large home, maintain his membership in his country club and continue to stable a horse, one that he spent little time riding. He felt trapped by the lifestyle he'd created and saw himself as someone who didn't have control of his choices. However, he was very much in control. Perhaps that control was more limited than in the past, but the point is that he still had command of many of these factors that he *believed* were trapping him.

When it comes to your career, where do you feel limited or trapped? Are you feeling that you are still in control of your career growth? What steps are you taking to use the power you have? Are you mapping out alternate plans and strategies within your organization? What conversations do you need to schedule and with whom?

If you have choices, you have control. Once you see yourself as a victim, you have given up your power and will not clearly see opportunities to redirect or rebuild your career path or your life. The key is to recognize change when it happens and then take steps to create a strategy to master it. Become a Ringmaster of *this* ring and you will find yourself far ahead of many of your coworkers!

When I think back to my days as a Human Resources professional, I recall many conversations initiated by employees. Most were regarding work relationships that went sour, a bad boss, demanding job duties, a promotion someone didn't get, lack of career opportunities and little or no pay raises. But what was at the real root of these issues? You guessed it – change. They were being impacted by the stress of change at work or lack of change in their daily responsibilities, and it came out as frustration with a manager (or in some other way that failed to get to the core reason). Usually, the real cause was either they didn't take appropriate steps to create positive change for themselves in the workplace or an inability to embrace change created by someone else (which we'll discuss more in the third ring).

The Ring Of Influence

This ring is all about working with others! Let's look at the three distinct ways you can master this too-often-dramatic ring.

1. CREATE AGREEMENT

After change comes to your organization, you have a limited window of time to put yourself in the position of being the connector of the group. This is the person who may enlighten others about the changes being made, help everyone come into agreement about new ways of working together and commit to unity around the change being made. Even if you are not leading the group, you can still be the catalyst that gets the group to determine how they deal collectively and positively with change.

2. EXHIBIT LEADERSHIP

You have the ability to bring others into a place of sharing, compromise and cohesive agreement. Leading within your team doesn't mean you have to be the official leader of the group. The important part is that you step forward to become the central figure who helps the larger group succeed in the face of change. The goal here is to actively influence everyone on the team to bring their best, realizing that what's important is that the organization run like a well-oiled machine. This may include helping team members get past who is right or wrong when conflict arises and instead focus on how to work productively, in harmony together.

3. BE THE EXAMPLE

This response to change is often overlooked, but is very valuable within organizations today. One of the best ways to influence others is to demonstrate that you are a person of integrity and character, even in the face of unexpected change. Remember that one of the best compliments you can receive in the workplace is a coworker who wants to emulate your actions. People who influence by example refrain from drawing quick conclusions, giving the benefit of the doubt to everyone in all situations. If you can keep emotional reactions in check and demonstrate reasonable responses to change, you can become a powerful and dynamic employee who has a powerful influence on others.

Ringmasters know the importance of influence. Creating interactions with others based on integrity and without judgment can increase your influence, whether you lead by creating agreement, through active leadership or simply by example.

The Ring Of Response

This ring is all about how you respond to the choices others are making – choices that impact your life and work. What are your emotional triggers? What are the things that get under your skin and cause you to clam up, speak out in frustration or go into denial? How quickly can you shift into a place of acceptance when an unexpected change barrels through your workplace?

This by far is the hardest ring to master! How well do you know yourself when it comes to embracing change? Can you identify your emotions quickly enough to plan your response? We will address your instinctive reactions to change in more detail toward the end of this book. You will also be given an opportunity to learn more about your responses to change by taking a simple online change behavior assessment.

MANAGER'S SPOTLIGHT

Getting to really know your team will be critical to your success as a manager of people. Defining expectations and the role in which you want each one to perform is so important in helping your team become Ringmasters and stay engaged. But statistics suggest that most managers aren't even considering the importance of engagement: 75% of leaders have no engagement plan or strategy even though 90% say engagement impacts business success (ACCOR). In addition, less than 50% of chief financial officers appear to understand the return on their investments in human capital (Accenture). Why is engaged "human capital" important? Well, the stats tell the story there, too:

▶ Actively disengaged employees cost the U.S. economy **$370 BILLION** annually. (GALLUP)

▶ **70% of engaged employees** indicate they have a good understanding of how to meet customer needs; only 17% of disengaged employees say the same. (WRIGHT MANAGEMENT)

▶ **78% of engaged employees** would recommend their company's products or services; only 13% of the disengaged would do the same. (GALLUP)

So where do you start in developing meaningful relationships with your employees and helping them comprehend the Three Rings Of Change?

The Ring Of Control

Begin by observing who takes on more responsibilities without saying, "This isn't my job!" These people will most likely *not* have a problem understanding the "Ring Of Control." The goal is to have everyone mentally embrace this within their own role and duties.

But unfortunately, a majority of your team likely do not understand the Ring Of Control. They place blame on others because they are unsettled in their role. It could be they don't like what they are doing, or simply don't have a good handle on things yet. Often, these people need more training or support. The faster they can be confident in their work and take full ownership of it, the more engaged they will be and the better it will be for everyone! So in order to help them understand the Ring Of Control, you must define clear and complete expectations.

The Ring Of Influence

Those times when your department needs to come together around a special project or implement something new is when you will find your real leaders. They understand the "Ring Of Influence" and how to best support the department or organization. These individuals understand how to build supportive relationships that get the job, task or project completed with as little stress as possible. But team members who don't understand the Ring Of Influence often lead to a lot of extra time and work for managers. Personality conflicts cost the manager time and money every day.

There's an old saying that goes, "I could be a great manager if it weren't for the people!" It's funny because it's kind of true. Wouldn't you say that getting everyone to do their job while getting along with each other is over half of what you do as a manager? If you have team chemistry problems like this on your team, you will need to 1) find ways to build a tight team, possibly through team-building exercises, and 2) spend one-on-one time with individuals so that you can get to the heart of any relationship conflict. You will read more concepts later in the book that discuss specific things you can do to build better relationships, such as implementing communication methods that will minimize cost and loss of time.

The Ring Of Response

The last ring will be more intuitively explored for managers toward the end of the book, featuring many helpful hints about what you can do to understand and help each employee have a positive response to unexpected change within the work environment.

The secret found in

STAR PERFORMERS

STRATEGY 1: KNOW YOUR PERSONAL BRAND

★ ★ ★ ★ ★ ★

In the early days of the circus you often found entire families performing. Take the popular flying trapeze family as an example. It was exciting for me to watch how each family member performed a different act or routine and then became known and remembered for doing it well. Although they all swung from bar to bar, each one perfected their own act – and built a reputation around that special ability. They found their natural talent and refined it.

That's what we have to do today in each of our careers. You must identify what comes naturally to you and then perfect it. Knowing this will help you focus your career growth and also develop your niche reputation. It's what will set you apart in your department or organization so that managers say, "Oh, give that project to Lois. No one could handle it quite like she does."

As you know, everyone in the workplace has a reputation, some good and some not so good. This reputation is essentially your brand, or at least a huge component of your brand. What are you known for? What problems do people turn to you to solve and how do you go about doing it? What tasks do people expect you to do well? Your title doesn't define your brand; the way you can answer those questions does.

But how do you begin to create (or recreate) your own reputation or "brand"? The process starts with looking at yourself. If you are like most people I work with, I'm guessing it's easier for you to name the things you're *not* good at, right? That's completely normal as it's much harder to focus on your strengths and even harder to articulate them so that they have real meaning.

If I asked you about the specific strengths you bring to your organization, how would you respond? That you're good with people? Dependable? Great at managing details? Those responses are fine, but what are they really saying about you? These are responses a lot of people could give. These are generic strengths that leave the listener thinking that there's nothing all that unique about what you can deliver.

Try this: Think about someone in your work environment who stands out. How would you describe them? Would it sound something like this?

"My coworker Owen is the best. He has an ability to analyze very complex financial data and simplify that data down to the basics, so everyone on the team can understand, and then go on to explain it to our clients."

Wouldn't you say this description of a professional strength has more meat to it? It's more defined and gives a better explanation of Owen's unique value to the organization.

So the challenge I'm giving you is to develop personal branding statements that tell the listener specifically how *you* work and how your efforts, output or methods are invaluable. If you have trouble knowing where to start, think about what comes naturally to you. I could learn how to work with data and numbers better than I do right now, but it will never be something that comes naturally for me – but that's just me!

What's Your DNA?

Here's another way to look at identifying your brand. You have probably heard someone play the piano and could see that they knew how to read music and play the notes consistently. But have you ever heard someone who *really* knows how to tickle the ivory? The experience changes your frame of reference for what you call a good pianist versus a great one! It's usually easy to see when someone with a natural talent is doing what they do best, taking real satisfaction in it.

The point is simple: If you look only at your *ability* to do a job, then your true greatness won't shine. You may have a reputation for doing many things well. However, if you are honest with yourself, some of those tasks may not give you satisfaction. You may not get energy or excitement from doing them. You have to separate ability from passion!

You've probably heard debates about nature versus nurture, and in a career, nature is so key. You have to identify your natural responses. What are the things you do well almost without thinking *and* take pleasure in doing? I call this your DNA: Defined Natural Ability.

When you define yourself only by titles and skills, the danger is that you might be heading for career burnout. You have the skills to do the job, but it's not your true DNA. If you base your career choice solely on the fact that you have the skills to do the job, you're forcing a career fit. Just because you might have the skills to haul trash doesn't mean a career in waste management is your destiny, does it? That's no criticism of trash haulers. For some people operating a truck of that size and power or being in a job that takes them outdoors every day is indeed what they love! But you get the point. Just because you can do it doesn't mean you were *meant* to do it.

WHY YOUR BRAND MATTERS

Your brand is what defines you in the workplace. How your DNA and abilities fit together to show the unique value you bring to the organization is your brand. When you align your brand with your job and its roles, you have a real reason to jump out of bed in the morning and go to work! You have lasting satisfaction and a sense of purpose because you know you're doing what you're meant to be doing, and that you're making an impact doing it.

Armed with the knowledge of your brand, you can grow with an organization and earn promotions that continue to build on your brand. This is part of what contributes to people developing a niche in their fields and becoming the go-to expert on that topic within their organization. Daniel Pink, author of the book *Drive*, states that three factors motivate us:

I believe that once you know your brand, you can become a master, doing something that gives you purpose – and *that* in and of itself brings about autonomy!

Some of you may already have a real sense of satisfaction and purpose in your job, but you can't necessarily put a finger on why you feel that way. We'll talk about another reason it's important that you define your brand in the last chapter in the book. So let me just say this for now: Nothing ever remains the same. Change is coming. When it does, will you have the right measurement tools in place to direct or transition your brand and your career in a changing environment?

How To Identify Your Brand

What we all have in common is an important personal challenge to figure out how to make a living while making a difference in our worlds. To do that, we need to understand and answer the "Why, How and What" in our careers.

Your **Why** is the belief, purpose and/or cause you live for.

Your **How** is what makes the way you work unique to you.

Your **What** is your specific career focus and experience.

Once you determine these, you're on your way to understanding your brand. The next step is articulating it.

The Branding Statement

It's imperative that you don't just *think* about these concepts but actually take the time to write out your brand statements. Having clarity about your personal brand will help you make organizational change an opportunity for, rather than an obstacle to, your career growth.

But how do you get to a great brand statement? What does one look like? I'll show you some great examples of branding statements shortly, but first there's something I need to be clear about: A branding statement is **NOT** an achievement. Branding statements broadly promote what makes you unique, where your achievements prove your brand is true and real. Branding statements aren't about a specific duty included as part of your job.

But achievements *do support* your branding statement. So in a way, you need to think through your achievements before you can fully craft your branding statement. I recommend starting by listing achievements from your life that you're really proud of and enjoyed doing. Some should be work-related, but you should also include those achievements that show up outside the walls of work, such as in your social or family life. Remember that with personal branding, the magic comes from *how* you work to bring about results.

Tips on writing these achievement statements:

1 ▶ Start with an action word.

2 ▶ Be as specific as possible in stating the achievement.

3 ▶ Focus on what you did to achieve rather than just the end result.

Poor Example: *Understand how to research consumer segments.*

Better Example: *Conducted primary and secondary research with newborn parents coast-to-coast to identify unique insights that could be strategically linked to our product's objectives.*

Poor Example: *Developed software.*

Better Example: *Collaborated with our company's Market Research and Programmers to create a unique computer software product to sell to hospitals.*

Poor Example: *Experience in managing residential neighborhood construction.*

Better Example: *Hired and managed approximately 200 subcontractors and vendors while completing a new $2M neighborhood development project.*

Now you're ready to begin. There's no need to wait. List your proudest achievements here:

1. _____

_____

2. _____

_____

3. _____

_____

4. _____

_____

5. _____

   _____

6. _____

   _____

7. _____

   _____

8. _____

   _____

9. _____

   _____

10. _____

    _____

Now that you have listed these achievements, look back and notice the common themes. What is your usual approach as you work on projects? What role do you usually play when working with a group? What are you doing over and over again, and what value are you creating in doing so? This is where you will find your true brand that will carry you through your work and life every day!

I call this a branding statement, and as with achievement statements, there are three components to consider when developing yours:

1. An Action You're looking for words like *develop, lead, create, analyze.*

2. To Whom or What? To whom or to what are you doing the action? These are usually things like financial reports, vendors, systems or individuals.

3. That Produces What Value? What's the result you most often produce when you do this?

Now I should practice what I preach. Here are a few examples of branding statements that I've developed for myself as a Career Coach, Author and Speaker:

> *I have the ability to **Develop** processes and procedures for myself and others, in order to reach the established goal while bringing everyone into agreement in order to implement it.*

> *I have the ability to **Create** tools and materials that enable individuals to learn and develop strategies to manage the ever-changing landscape of their life and career.*

> *I have the ability to **Present** information to groups or large audiences that motivates them to take an action and that inspires their growth.*

The Rings In Action

THE RING OF CONTROL AND
THE RING OF INFLUENCE

When you identify your personal brand, you complete the first step in becoming a Ringmaster. You will know how to best control your career's direction by developing a tool that helps you engage with your superiors. This empowers you to be a part of their discussion, and influence what steps you can take together.

Action To Activ8

Develop at least three personal branding statements:

1. _____

_____

2. _____

_____

3. _____

_____

After you have identified a combination of branding statements, the last test is asking yourself, "Do I get energy doing this?" Sometimes we identify patterns that *don't* give us energy. You might find you do things better than others – but that in and of itself doesn't mean we use this ability to help determine how to direct our career.

Once you have identified those branding statements that give you energy, you will probably think of other achievements you didn't list before. Go ahead and add them!

Now that you've identified your brand, it's time to have a discussion with your VP, Director or Manager about how and where you bring the most value to the organization. You can then develop a career track that matches your DNA, not one just based on your skills. You might even develop new areas of interest that will benefit both you and your organization.

This action plan should be linked to the changes occurring in the organization. How can your brand align with where the company is going? How do you bring unique value to its future using the innate abilities represented in your branding statement?

Remember that changes in the organization may lead to changes in your role or duties. But your core brand and abilities are what can carry you to the next level and keep you not only *relevant* to the company's future, but *vital* to its success. Let's explore how you should think about your skill set in a changing world.

The Thumbtack Approach

There's an old saying in business: "If you're not growing and transforming, then you're losing business and heading backwards." That statement refers to companies, but the same goes for individuals. If you are not growing and learning something new, then you are too content with living in the status quo, waiting for *someone else* to change your world. Wouldn't you want to direct change before someone else does?

It then becomes a matter of knowing how to make that change without pigeonholing yourself. And that's where the Thumbtack Approach comes in. We'll use a metaphor for three ways to attach one material to another – a nail, a sticker and a thumbtack.

The first image you see is of a nail. By itself, it's pointed so that when you nail it into wood it's secure and hard to remove. The nail delves into one very specific area and represents being a niche expert in your field, with real depth of knowledge. This is someone you might call a "guru" in a specific area of focus.

Let's think about the sticker. It is broad and thin, representing someone who is a "generalist" with limited but useful knowledge in many areas related to their field. Generalists know enough about the multiple areas of their department so that they can be flexible and fill in for someone who is out of the office at any time. Managers can conveniently move them around as needed, even though they don't really have a specific expertise.

A thumbtack is both. It has qualities of the nail and the sticker. This person has both a broad knowledge of topics related to their work, but also in-depth knowledge and skills in at least one relevant discipline. Why would anyone want to be a thumbtack in this metaphor? Because when a company is reorganizing the department or looking to lay off part of their workforce, they'll most likely value someone who is both a generalist and a niche expert. These people have more to offer the organization because they don't have just one skill, nor are they limited in their knowledge of related functions. In other words, as a thumbtack, they are *pretty good at everything* and *great at something*!

The Ring In Action

THE RING OF CONTROL

The strategy here is to develop your skills so that you have a good working knowledge of your department or discipline. This might open the door for you to work with management on specific goals and projects that you can lead or in which you can become a niche expert. It's your job to ask the questions and be aware of what the organization is focused on accomplishing. Opportunities are often right in front of us, however we fail to see them because we think the next big opportunity only comes in the form of a promotion. Get involved and be willing to stretch yourself beyond your immediate job duties.

Actions To Activ8

What are the steps you need to take to develop your career thumbtack? Identify the one area where you can be "the guru" while listing the other areas where you can generally perform well (or, if not, the areas in which you need to develop general skills in order to remain relevant and valuable).

_____

_____

_____

_____

_____

_____

_____

_____

_____

_____

MANAGER'S
SPOTLIGHT

Per a recent article in the *Seattle Post-Intelligencer*, when organizations were surveyed and asked, "To what extent does your company know your strengths and put your strengths into play every day?" only 20% of people agree that their organizations do this to a great extent. That means 80% of employees feel that their managers and teams don't recognize or utilize their strengths well!

This is a two-way street. Both the employee and the manager need to make an effort in identifying the employee's brand.

But before you the manager can start talking about how your team members can or should identify their brands within your department, you need to lead by example. If you don't walk the walk, don't talk the talk. It won't work and you'll lose respect. Remember that these tools and approaches not only strengthen your individual team members' abilities, but can help them cope with the changes in your organization.

If you can define your personal brand, then you can help others who report to you do the same thing. Start observing where each of your employees shines and finds enjoyment. It would help to have regular meetings with them and talk about what parts of their jobs they like most and least - you might be surprised at what you discover. For example, you might find that some of their issues stem from not feeling adequately trained or prepared. But you won't know until you ask.

Focus on building around their strengths because you will get more out of them as workers if they are using the innate skills that define their brands. Your job is not to develop employees who are perfect at everything. That's the old-school manager's way of thinking. Your job is to help them deepen the knowledge and expertise that will focus them on their natural strengths. If you want superstar performers, this is how you get them! Patience is required, but the end result is a team that is able to activate their abilities more easily and cope with change more readily.

ATTENTION, LADIES *and* GENTLEMEN

STRATEGY 2: DEVELOP A SOLID COMMUNICATION STRATEGY

★ ★ ★ ★ ★ ★

When a three-ring circus is in full swing, acts are changing right and left – and it's the Ringmaster's job to communicate to the audience what's happening and where to look next so that they can get the most from their experience.

With change comes the need for communication. They go hand in hand. A leader's challenge is to effectively communicate the change that has occurred or is about to occur. Whether officially in a position of leadership or simply one of the team, you have an opportunity to be a Ringmaster when it comes to how you deal with change and how to help others cope with it as well.

Repeat, Confirm, Clarify

Whether you're the one communicating the change or the one receiving the communication, the first rule is to *repeat, repeat, repeat*. You can't communicate too much when introducing a change of any kind. When I was working in corporate America, I made it a habit to repeat back to my boss what I thought I heard when defining what I was asked to implement or change moving forward. You might have heard me say, "To make sure I'm on the same page, what you're saying is… is that correct?"

Now, the "…" is where *confirming* and *clarifying* come into play. When repeating back to my bosses what I interpreted them to be saying, I confirmed deadlines and clarified how I would notify my boss once my action was completed, for instance. By doing this, I was able to guarantee that I wasn't misinterpreting any details or expectations.

A plan to *repeat, confirm, clarify* may sound simple, but it can be a challenge if you're in a rush to get back to a project or move on to the next one. It also gets more complicated when you go from one-on-one communication of change to one that involves a team dynamic.

The Consequences Of Bad Communication

Bad communication can ultimately lead to a poor bottom line, but the first signs usually come from strained employee relations. So much of what I've experienced around employee relation breakdowns comes from a lack of communication. I used to moderate conversations between employees and try to resolve their issues with each other, focusing on how we could build a healthier coworker relationship. But what I found was that the problem often fell into two areas that needed clarification: individual roles and goals.

Lack of clear communication around the expectations of roles and goals creates problems in personal relationships as well as professional ones. Take Stan for example. While doing some consulting work for his boss, I started to get to know Stan. It wasn't long before he came to me with a dilemma:

"David, you're good at this problem-solving thing. So can you explain what happened to me this morning? While having breakfast with my wife, she said to me, 'Stan, how come you never buy me flowers or take me out to buy a new dress?' I looked at her and could tell something was bothering her, so I responded, 'That's not a problem.' I got up from my chair and pulled out my wallet and said, 'I just went to the bank yesterday. Here's my wallet – take what you want and go buy yourself something pretty.' But she stopped and stared at me with a look that I can only describe as disgust. She took all of the money out of my wallet as she shook her head and left the room! I don't have a clue about what happened or what went wrong! Can you help me understand?"

The problem was that Stan didn't understand what his wife was really trying to communicate. He didn't realize that she was speaking in "code" that she thought he would be able to interpret. After I told Stan that his wife wasn't really asking for the money and that she wanted him to show her some attention, his face lit up as he exclaimed, "Why didn't she just say that?!"

The point is that when it comes to expectations about roles and goals during an organizational change, you must be 100% clear and to the point. You never know if one of your team members is like Stan: not able to read between the lines.

Three Considerations When Communicating Change

But what if the person trying to communicate change is NOT being 100% clear and to the point? As Stan learned the hard way, it's often our job as the message receivers to ask questions so that we understand the goals and what role we need to play. Whether you're the message sender or receiver, there are three points to walk away understanding, two of which I've hopefully already made:

1
GOALS

2
ROLES

3
RELATIONSHIPS

I've learned that if you can get everyone to see the overall goal, and to clearly understand each other's roles and how they work together, good relationships will usually follow!

The Ring In Action

THE RING OF INFLUENCE

This strategy is about how you effectively communicate with coworkers, project leads and others. You must be active and set goals that will impact everyone within your department or organization. How will you be a catalyst, driving everyone toward next steps collectively? How will you lead, whether you are managing the project or not? Trust me, everyone – higher-ups and your peers – will take note and watch the way you participate in bringing harmony to a goal or project. When you are a Ringmaster, you will often be admired from a distance and others will want to emulate you.

Action To Activ8

Where is the confusion happening within your role or the roles of your coworkers? What can you do to help bring clarity to the goal or roles?

_____

_____

_____

_____

_____

MANAGER'S
SPOTLIGHT

If you can learn to communicate change clearly - both one-on-one and to a team - it will pay off for you and for the organization big time! Studies have shown that communication is the most common thing managers do, spending 60% to 80% of their time communicating with their teams. This could be face-to-face, over the phone or via e-mail. So clearly, communication is key. But the problem is this: Stats suggest most managers are bad communicators.

In one relevant survey, 86% of managers thought they were good communicators, but only 17% said their managers actually communicated effectively. Another substantial survey uncovered that only 14% of people rated managers in their organization as "good" or "very good." So what tangible steps can a manager take to beat the odds?

Let's start with a story. I remember working with my manager years ago, sitting in a small room with a large dry-erase board, talking about our processes. First, we identified what our overall departmental goal was and how our roles were created to support it. We then started drafting what each role within the department was supposed to accomplish, and how each person was handing off the work to the next coworker in the process. We created a massive flow chart and got really clear about who did what and when they did it. It took several weeks to develop, but in doing so we found where the gaping holes were in our processes. We started using the *repeat, confirm, clarify* communication method when a new employee joined the team. Someone walked them through the processes in detail, and the result was that the processes continued to stick!

Conversely, a former client of mine working in New York has called me several times in frustration, describing the stress she is under because her manager is not clearly communicating or defining how her employees should work together, or who should do what. The consequence is that deadlines are never met and everyone is looking to leave the company.

Her manager's solution has been to hire more contract workers to help the team crawl out of the crater she's created, mistakenly thinking the problem is about needing more workers instead of effectively defining roles and processes. If the problems are not resolved, the company is threatening to shut down the whole department and hire an outside agency to manage the business, while they regroup and rebuild the department from the ground up! Consider that a cautionary tale of what could happen if you don't take seriously communicating change and clarifying goals, roles and responsibilities.

DON'T HIDE
from the
SPOTLIGHT

★ ★ ★ ★ ★ ★

While acrobats, jugglers and circus clowns do the same act night in, night out, over and over, great circus folks never allow themselves to settle for a lackluster performance. They record how they performed (be it mentally or literally through video cameras), looking for opportunities to be even better the next time. In other words, star performers make it count every time!

This is a behavior that you should emulate in all your duties, especially when organizational change is on the horizon. You need to be documenting your actions so that you can look back to them in any instant and prove what you did and why it added value to your organization. Most importantly, it will show you how you can build on past performance going forward.

Why is this so important? From my experience as a Career Coach, I've learned it's hard for people to retrieve accomplishments simply from memory. So when the time comes for a self-review or to reinforce to the boss why they add value (and shouldn't even be considered in the upcoming layoff!), they aren't armed with the arsenal of achievements they need to prove their worth. But those who wrote down their accomplishments have them ready to position themselves for success. But if they hadn't written them down, it could be as if they never happened!

The other problem I often find is that some people remember a big accomplishment they worked on as a team, but have a hard time identifying what part of the project they personally took ownership of. If you write down what you are doing in the moment, then you can remember *every* aspect of it, including your specific contribution to the effort.

How To Start Tracking Accomplishments

So how are you tracking your progress? Are you preparing for your performance review? Are you taking ownership of what you are doing?

There are numerous ways you can do this. Here are some tips:

> ▶ Create a dated spreadsheet or Word document (or whatever program you find most user-friendly) to capture everything you are doing. Keep it updated.
>
> ▶ Use your computer calendar to record a reminder of what you did. Many calendar programs feature a task list you can use.
>
> ▶ Keep your list of written achievements handy in a file or desktop folder so you can review them at a moment's notice if need be.

At the end of the month, review and edit your list of accomplishments. If you want to make sure that you get an "Exceeds Expectations" rating on your review each year, track whether or not you are meeting the basic requirements of the job *first* and then you can add the extra accomplishments (those additional projects or tasks that went above and beyond your current responsibilities.) This will help your boss evaluate what specific things you have accomplished and brought to the department, not to mention the overall organization.

Now I know for some of you the perceived monotony and detail of tracking your accomplishments feels like getting a root canal! It may never be completely painless, but if you can make organizing your accomplishments part of a daily or weekly routine, you'll find it a lot easier. Doing it in bite sizes – even 10 minutes a week – will pay off! The next section will outline a more detailed method of keeping track of what you do that adds value to your organization.

Keeping Your Accomplishments Organized

Keeping up files on your desktop or simply listing what you've done in a Word document is a great way to start. But once you get going, you'll likely realize you need a more detailed way to organize all of the accomplishments you're tracking.

The challenge is prioritizing the projects when deadlines or the scope of work change daily, weekly and sometimes by the hour. I'm big on visual aids, so I created an ongoing spreadsheet where I can prioritize each project on a dime; I've color-coded them according to where I am with that specific project.

WHITE means this is an ongoing project. (No real beginning with no end.)

GREEN means I need to start this project and post a possible start date.

YELLOW means I've already started the project but still have steps to finish. This is also where I list the details needed to finish the project.

RED means I have finished the project and met the objective. It's officially an accomplishment!

The Ring In Action

THE RING OF INFLUENCE

This is all about tracking what projects you took the lead on and nailed.
The real value here is you have proof of times you've accomplished
something, empowering YOU to direct the conversation and influence
your managers as you share your accomplishments with them.

Action To Activ8

What are you committing to do so that you can identify and track your
achievements? Set a date for when you will start tracking!

_____

_____

_____

_____

_____

_____

MANAGER'S SPOTLIGHT

One thing I think we forget is not everyone learns and processes information the same way. I'm dyslexic, which results in me processing things in a way that's very different from others around me. I learn best by doing, not talking. The hands-on approach has always been my best learning method, rather than reading a book about "how to."

I share this because the best way for your employees to learn from tracking their accomplishments won't be universal. One thing that separates good teachers from great is that great ones often tailor an individual approach to each of their students. They know how to get the best performance out of them. So put on your teacher's hat and find ways that work for each employee when tracking their progress and achievements.

I once saw a report that suggested you ask yourself the following questions to determine if you're doing a good job helping your team track their successes:

- ☐ Do my employees know how I judge and measure their performance?

- ☐ Do I provide and encourage individual development with training and educational programs?

- ☐ Do I trust my employees and rely upon their knowledge?

- ☐ Do I let employees make decisions?

- ☐ Do I have timely, accurate, open, two-way communication with my employees?

If you're not answering "yes" to many of the above questions, you might need to reevaluate the way you're helping your team track their success.

And remember to keep an open mind in your approach. If there is a team project, then assign someone in the group the responsibility of capturing what specific duties have been completed by each member of the team. Then everyone gets a copy for their records!

For some, that may mean they need to partner up with another coworker and hold each other accountable for tracking their accomplishments. Think outside the box for each person. It will save you time on the back end, and come review time you will have all the information you need right at your fingertips!

WARNING: PERFORMANCES MAY VARY

STRATEGY 4: UNDERSTAND THE REWARD SYSTEM IN YOUR CORPORATE CULTURE

★ ★ ★ ★ ★ ★

Not every circus is the same. In fact, not every circus performance of every circus is the same – just look at the wide variety of Cirque du Soleil shows! But that's the point. Whether it's Cirque du Soleil's original show, *The Beatles LOVE* show or *Zarkana* show, each has its own culture and attracts and rewards different kinds of performers.

I often talk with individuals who are not satisfied with where they are going in their careers, complaining about how their managers don't appreciate how *they* perform. But their problems may stem from a mismatch that existed from their first day with the company. They never considered the company's culture before taking the job, much less when trying to move ahead. Would a world-class acrobat blindly accept a role in an animal-focused circus? No. So why should you accept a job before considering the culture within which you'll be expected to perform?

Pay Attention To What Work Environments Reward

The leadership within a company drives its culture. So the question to ask yourself (and to always keep asking) is this: "What behaviors does the company and its leadership reward?" You will quickly find out the company "currency" (meaning what makes someone valuable) when this question is answered. You'll thereby discover what it takes for you to stand out, as well as whether or not the organization is really living up to its mission, vision and value statements. Some examples will really help illustrate this point.

I recently met a very successful salesperson – we'll call him Dave. He was hitting all the numbers and kept his head down, staying out of company politics, focusing on scaling the next mountain. But despite all of that, Dave was given the pink slip. Understandably, he was confused since he routinely surpassed his sales goals. But after we talked further about his role, I found out that he wasn't recording and keeping accurate information and data on his processes and sales. He was unpredictable. Sure, Dave's sales numbers were good, but everyone else was running around having to track his numbers. This was not a corporate culture that accepted, much less rewarded, letting the details fall through the cracks in exchange for better numbers. He was a results-oriented performer failing in a process-oriented culture. But Dave's not unique. Many of us focus so much on how to build our careers that we forget to look up and make sure that *how* we work may actually be the thing the organization rewards.

I also worked with an executive who was employed by a global organization. We'll call him Toby. He had been there for over 15 years and had been promoted many times, ultimately landing an executive role. So what he experienced next caught him by surprise. You see, Toby was known for his ability to take large amounts of financial data and condense it to easy-to-understand but meaningful applications. He really loved this part of his job and was rewarded for his performance in this area – until the organization decided to restructure several departments.

Toby now reported to someone new. He continued to do what he had always done before, but this time he noticed a change in the responses to his efforts. There was a new reward system in place. In the past, Toby had challenged the status quo (including his management) when looking for the most effective approach to solving or finding a solution around efficiencies. But the new boss didn't like his aggressive approach and began limiting his job duties. The manager began bringing in new employees from other departments. After a year of this, Toby found himself stuck in an office with very little interaction with others. He was dying a slow professional death. He had not realized earlier that when the new boss took over, the culture he knew had dramatically changed, and that it was *his* job to adapt to that change. And that's a lesson we all need to understand and embrace.

UNDERSTAND "FIT"

Here's a little insider HR secret: When someone is brought in to be interviewed face-to-face, most of the time HR or management have usually already concluded that the interviewee has the skills to do the job. This is especially true if the person is an internal candidate. The decision often boils down to fit.

Here are just some of the "fit" questions they ask themselves:

☐ Does this candidate fit our organization, department and overall culture?

☐ Do they think like we think?

☐ Do they work appropriately with authority?

☐ Do they stand for the same ideals we do?

If you've ever been on the employer's side of the hiring process, you already know this is true. You've probably met a candidate that you think is a good fit, even if they don't have all of the skill sets yet. You may have even hired them, thinking, "I really like how this person thinks. I can train them to learn the skills they are lacking." This is a demonstration of how much an employer can value fit, even when job skills are not perfect for the position.

The Kinds Of Cultures

The speed of change that occurs within organizations has increased almost universally due to a number of factors, including the rise of the Internet and new opportunities for companies to gain market advantage if they move quickly. But with this change in how companies do business comes new expectations of leaders and workers. The currency the organization values is a set of behaviors they reward. It's your job to find out what kind of culture you're working within so that you can adapt, shine and reap the rewards. The faster you learn about these kinds of cultures and make your own adjustments, the sooner they pay off.

That being said, here are some cultures to consider when trying to identify the one in which you're working. I go much more in depth about each of these, as well as other cultures, in my book *From Cornered To Corner Office.* activ8careers.com/from-cornered-to-corner-office

THE GRINDSTONE CULTURE

This is often an ideal culture for high achievers, as the name of the game is hard work. This type of organization values people who don't mind late hours to get the job done. This is a fast-paced environment where change occurs often.

WHAT THEY REWARD: Taking initiative to get the job done, long hours, embracing challenges.

THE "AHA" CULTURE

This culture is all about new ways of thinking. It thrives on innovation. Employees are free to speak their minds and share opinions. The company is more likely to embrace ideas that challenge the status quo. Individuals who thrive on being creative fit naturally in this kind of environment.

WHAT THEY REWARD: Coming up with new ideas and approaches, proposing a different solution, doing something no one else thought about doing.

THE PROCESS CULTURE

This culture loves structure. Well-defined job duties and procedures for each role are mandatory. Those in a Process Culture are great at measuring systems, productivity and services. They don't like coloring outside the lines, but know what they do well.

WHAT THEY REWARD: Developing user-friendly systems, processes to manage new business opportunities, better ways of measuring outcomes.

The Ring In Action

THE RING OF CONTROL

You are responsible to figure out how to work best with those you report to. If you don't understand this concept, you might as well walk around work blindfolded and hope you find success. Every corporate culture and manager has expectations about how you present yourself and your work within the organization. And YOU are in charge of taking control and making sure you live according to the culture. Now, some of you may be thinking, "But I can change the culture for the better!" That very well may be the case. But don't rush it. Prove that you can live in their culture before you try to evolve it.

Action To Activ8

What kind of culture are you working in now? What behavior does your company really reward? What is it that you need to work on in order to achieve the "fit" within the culture? Keep in mind that company cultures may change significantly over time, so the answers to these questions may be different in the future.

_____

_____

_____

_____

_____

_____

_____

_____

_____

_____

MANAGER'S SPOTLIGHT

A report toward the beginning of the recent recession stated that 60% of people intended to leave their job. Why? Because employees are discontent, and disengaged because they don't feel they can express their ideas to their managers.

The most surprising thing about this is that it comes amidst a huge economic downfall with unemployment statistics moving upward. It's clear that "just having a job" isn't enough no matter how bad things look. So as a manager, you can't sit back and assume people will be content. You must ask yourself if you're building a team-based workplace environment where people will *want* to be every day.

When it comes to culture, *you* set the tone! Your behavior, along with the behaviors you reward on your team, dictate your department's culture. Large companies have an overarching culture, but you also might find other types of "mini cultures" within the organization that reward different behaviors. The culture that works best for your department's needs is up to you to discover and create. Sometimes your industry and/or department responsibilities may dictate *some* of the culture, such as finance or accounting-related fields where accuracy and details will always be rewarded. The important thing to do as a manager is to make sure everyone understands what's expected of them, and in what fashion you want it delivered.

PLANNING
for your
STARDOM
into the future

★ ★ ★ ★ ★ ★

Do you think that a star performer in a circus stops trying to improve their act once it gets "pretty good"? Of course not! They set new goals for themselves. Tightrope walkers place their rope a few feet higher. Trapeze artists try an even more dangerous stunt. Lion tamers teach their cats new tricks. They all know that if they reach their goal, they'll have a new attraction on their hands, opening up the opportunity to shine in a whole new light.

So that leads to the question – where are you going within your organization? What are your long-term goals? For some, it's about learning more techniques or developing a new computer skill.

For others, it's about career advancement, greater responsibilities within the organization and climbing the corporate ladder.

How Change Impacts Your Goals

It's a fact, not simply a cliché. What you know today will not be enough to take you to where you need to go tomorrow!

Whether we like it or not, job roles grow, develop into new roles, and sometimes are even eliminated and replaced by something that didn't exist before. You can't afford to assume that doing a good job means you have job security. Time doesn't stand still, and neither will your job. You are not helping yourself or the organization if you are not looking for ways to grow. And a lot of that has to do with predicting how you think your job will change in coming years.

But what if you aren't concerned with how your job will change because you aren't sure where you want to be in five to 10 years? After all, our passions and interests do evolve. If you don't know where you want to be in a decade, start by listing 10 or so job titles that intrigue you. These might be job titles that have nothing to do with your current job, or they might be within your own department and in the same area of focus, just a different role (just know that if the job title is not within your expertise, you are truly exploring a new focus, one you most likely will not be able to move into right away).

Look at your list and highlight the five job titles that most interest you. From that five, circle the two that interest you most. Now comes the fun part – getting to truly understand those roles. The best place to start is to talk with people currently doing the job in which you're interested. You can never get a more accurate account of what the job is like than when you talk with someone who is doing it! By this simple process of talking to others, you'll likely gather enough information about what you would need to do to be considered for the position, so write everything down! Put together a list of certifications, skill sets, or even more schooling if that's required for you to take this career path.

But make sure that the payoff for what you are pursuing is worth the effort. What I mean is that you need to be certain that most of the duties, skills and goals associated with this role are things that will give you energy. Just having the ability to do the job isn't enough. Measure it against the personal branding statements you created. Since your brand is about what comes naturally to you (your "DNA") you want to make sure it's not far off. If you do indeed decide to pursue something new, hopefully you have a manager who won't take it personally, especially if the change would mean a transfer within your current organization. There are guidelines within every organization about requesting a transfer, so make sure you play by the rules and follow the guidelines provided by your HR department. You don't want to burn any bridges!

The Ring In Action

THE RING OF CONTROL

I often find people feel more comfortable and do better when someone else gives them a nudge, setting them in the right direction. That's understandable. We live in a world where everyone goes through 12 years of school to earn their diploma and then goes to a college that maps out their schedule to attain a certification or degree. So, you see, we're used to patterns and are comfortable looking to others to plan and direct us, which spills over to our careers. The reality is that you have had more control of your destiny than you might realize. You have been making choices all along. The more you direct your career, the more satisfied you will be, and the less chance you will have of blaming everyone else for an unhealthy career focus.

Action To Activ8

List some of your immediate or short-term goals:

1. _____

2. _____

3. _____

4. _____

5. _____

List your long-term goals:

1. _____

2. _____

3. _____

4. _____

5. _____

Now look back and follow the process I outlined above. If you always have a goal to pursue, you will be more likely to achieve positive change – a sure sign you're on your way to becoming a Ringmaster!

MANAGER'S SPOTLIGHT

Some managers try to hang on to good people too long. After all, who wants to lose a star performer they helped create? Just understand ahead of time that some of your star employees will stay and others will go. I've been in organizations where managers have the reputation of helping their staff develop and grow. They rarely have to look at external candidates to fill positions because internal team members are constantly encouraging other employees to request a transfer to their departments when an opportunity opens up. They have such a good reputation for developing and growing their people that they almost exclusively attract those who have what it takes to be star performers.

Your team needs good guidance and a reliable, inspiring mentor. Be committed to helping each of your team members find ways to grow professionally and personally. Working together, you can start identifying long-range goals. If you're part of setting those goals, you have a personal stake in your team member and they know it - which drives expectations, loyalty and a healthier work environment. Remember that you might have some people on your team who don't want to climb the ladder, so their goals may be about deepening their skill sets or developing into a specialist/expert in a niche area.

A lot of this begins with knowing how to write good, tangible goals with your employee. This is important so that you can really settle into your mentor role and help them continually assess if they're on the path to reaching those goals. I recently read a *Wall Street Journal* article that called out seven great tips to consider when writing goals:

1. Goals must align with the organization's mission and strategy.

2. They must be clear and easy to understand.

3. They must be accepted and recognized as important by everyone who will have to implement them.

4. Progress towards goals must be measurable.

5. Goals must be framed in time, with clear beginning and ending points.

6. They should be supported by rewards.

7. They should be challenging, but achievable.

When you're clear about your employee's goals and the path through which they can achieve them, you've taken the first great step in becoming a mentor.

The
BIG-TOP DOESN'T RAISE ITSELF

STRATEGY 6: ...WORK THE PLAN

★ ★ ★ ★ ★ ★

Simply setting the goal isn't enough. When the circus comes to town, the "raising of the tent" is a big deal. The circus manager and ground crew have a very specific goal – to get the tent up – but they also have a very specific set of action steps to do so successfully and safely.

The performers have a similar mentality. An acrobat whose goal is a new stunt doesn't just say, "I want to do *that* stunt next," and then do it. They create a strategy and action steps to work their way up to the stunt, finding safe ways to rehearse it and master it before they ever try it in front of a real audience.

You need to do the same thing. Creating an actionable plan to reach your goal is essential.

This is especially the case if your real-world experience doesn't link directly with your college degree. Over the years, I've met hundreds of people who have a career they love, but a degree that has nothing to do with it! So how did they get to where they are today?

There's one common thing in every one of these people's stories. They found connections and identified action steps to make it a reality. Here are some examples of the kinds of steps I'm talking about.

FIND A MENTOR

Hypothetically, let's say you decide that over the next few years you want to get into marketing and move into a Brand Manager role. Your next step should be to find a brand management professional who can mentor you into this role. Look for the best in an organization and learn from them. Actively spend more time with them. Find ways to insert yourself into their tasks, helping them solve problems or simply adding value to their department.

PUT IN THE HOURS

Once you find your mentor and begin building a relationship, next comes the hard part. Assuming you're not quitting your "old" job first, you have to diligently keep up with your regular workload while at the same time adding more *new* duties to your plate (that's likely already full!). You can't shirk your other responsibilities while pursuing a new career path; it won't look good if you get fired for not doing your job because you were looking for greener pastures! So know ahead of time that you might have to come in early or stay late in order to make pursuit of a new opportunity really work.

DEVELOP A TIME LINE AND MEASUREMENTS

What's realistic? Can you be fully prepared to transition into a new role and do it well by next month? Next year? Make sure you communicate to your boss what you want to accomplish for the organization. Have regular meetings (at least once a quarter) to talk about your progress. Telling your boss when and how you envision transitioning over to a new department isn't enough. I recommend finding a documentation tool of some kind that you and your manager can use to measure your progress (for example, an Excel document that tracks experiences you need to have before you transition). Then set some goals and time lines. Understand that no one can predict the exact time you might get the green light to move over to the new department. But once the goals you and your manager set have been reached and the opportunity arises, you'll be ready. Some of the best advice I got was from a VP I reported to years ago who said that I shouldn't ask for a promotion but rather just start doing the job, then she would have to figure out how to make the promotion happen.

IDENTIFY INDUSTRY TRENDS

A great way to expand your networking base is to join specialized professional organizations and associations. I recommend setting up Web alerts for news on your specific industry interest. You should also consider taking classes to attain necessary certification or learn new technologies. This way, when the time is right to actually start your new role, you can have a head start.

BECOME A NICHE EXPERT WITHIN THE MARKETPLACE

As you explore a new career path, look for special projects or special knowledge of the industry that will add unique value to an organization. With this approach, both the employee and organization win. I talked about this already when I explained the thumbtack approach.

NEVER STOP NETWORKING

As I tell my clients, your connections (or "network" if you prefer) are most crucial to building your career, and that includes when you're developing a strategy to reach your goals. To best position yourself for success, you need to connect with, learn from, and add value to internal work groups and individuals who can help you along. But you should also focus on connections outside of your current company or organization. Not necessarily because you're looking to leave your job, but getting involved with experts outside of your organization will give you new perspectives.

Social media is a great way to do this. Blogs, career forums, LinkedIn and LinkedIn groups, Twitter – these tools aren't just for job seekers anymore. Today, social media enables you to learn from others about career development and even position yourself as a thought leader in a certain industry or topic. It's a great way to find out what the latest trends are in the market and what you should take back to share with your organization. Just keep in mind that some companies have guidelines around using social media, so read the company policy.

The Ring In Action

THE RING OF CONTROL

This is about taking that first step! You don't have to sprint into deepening your niche or identifying the next career opportunity, you just need to get moving forward. If you consistently push yourself and commit to continual growth for you and the organization, after six months, I guarantee you will be surprised when you look back and see how much you've grown.

Action To Activ8

What specific strategies will you put in place that will assist you in reaching your goals?

_____

_____

_____

_____

_____

MANAGER'S
SPOTLIGHT

Obviously, you can't always promise the exact time you'll be able to promote an employee or transition them to a new department. Your best practice here is having open and honest conversations along the way. Statistics show that if an employee feels their manager treats them well and has a genuine interest in them, they will stay in a job even if they could go somewhere else with higher pay. So take the time and invest in your employees. Try to meet more than once a year to review their performance. Remember what we say in HR: Everything you communicate in your review should have been communicated at some point prior to review day. Surprising an employee with suggestions or concerns about their performance will no doubt have them asking, "Why are you just NOW telling me this?"

Again, this goes back to properly setting goals. If your employees understand what's expected of them, they're going to do a better job, and that will be reflected in your bottom line. Not too long ago Harris Research conducted a study for Stephen Covey (of Franklin Covey), to understand how to better lead an organization toward successful strategy execution, much of which centered around reaching goals:

▶ Only 30% of companies actually reach their goals.

▶ Only 15% of employees can identify their company's goals and priorities.

▶ 51% of employees don't understand what they need to do to meet the goals.

▶ 51% work on things that are urgent but not important.

▶ 81% feel no ownership in getting the goals completed.

Imagine what a little solid communication around goals could do for your organization!

So what are you doing? Are you partnering with your executives or the CEO in your organization? Have you been putting together succession plans? Are you setting advanced goals and growing the organization that in turn also grows your staff? When you can answer "yes" to those questions, you'll see a big positive difference.

The
AUDITIONS COUNT

★ ★ ★ ★ ★ ★

Even the most seemingly timeless circus acts know that nothing lasts forever. All performers know that they must continually develop and perfect new acts that they can take to the next audition. Just like them, you have to stay relevant, sometimes even reinventing yourself – and you have to be able to know how to show off your skills in an audition.

Of the many crafts one must know to be a career Ringmaster, the art of the job interview is one of the hardest. Let's say you're one of several candidates for a possible promotion. You have worked for this organization for several years. You know all the right people and are confident that the job is yours. However, when you enter the room and the interview begins, you find yourself not as prepared as you thought you would be. Before you know it, you're talking in circles, going on and on, realizing you're still answering a question they asked 10 minutes ago! If you're like most people, you've probably experienced something similar to this at some unfortunate point.

No matter how well you know the decision makers and how much of a "shoe-in" you think you are, winging a job interview is never a good idea, especially when just a *little* preparation can help you ace it! Here's the secret to success: Behavioral interviews are made up of five basic questions that can easily and strategically be prepared for. So what are we waiting for?!

1. THE **VALUE** QUESTION

"Why should I hire you?" When you're asked this straightforward, open-ended question, start with your brand. Showcase what you're known for in the workplace and what you're passionate about. Include the specific patterns that outline how you work and the value you bring – the things that ultimately set you apart. Explain that when you use these patterns, you always bring value to the organization.

2. THE **ABILITY** QUESTION

"Can you give me a specific example of how you multitasked while in your last job?" Specific ability questions like this are based around your skills and are meant to probe to see if you can do the job. I recommend you answer these questions with this three-part formula: what you did, how you did it and the result. But the trick is identifying those three aspects of the formula and having them at the ready *before* you walk into the interview!

3. THE **FIT** QUESTION

"Why do you want to work here?" This may surprise you based on the culture section earlier in the book, but the way to answer this is by stating that you don't fully know yet. Why? Because unless you've worked there, how can you *really* know?! But don't stop there. Continue with a transition along the lines of, "Here's what I do know from your web site, contacts who work here…" etc. Finish by asking, "How accurate am I?" That way you'll show how you fit without looking presumptuous. Now, if you're an internal candidate, the way you answer this question needs to be more about how you will fit naturally with the current team, management and dynamics. Leverage the fact that you have this insider information through a personal, insightful point of view.

4. THE **WEAKNESS** QUESTION

"What's your biggest weakness?" This one always trips people up. The key is not reinforcing a "weakness," but rather something you've learned. A simple transitional phrase is, "Here's what I've learned... ." This way, you're turning a negative into a positive! Then tell your "learning" story using positive information, followed up with something to the effect of, "Would knowing something like this from experience be valuable in this position?"

5. THE **NEGOTIATION** QUESTION

"What are your salary requirements?" If you're an **internal candidate**, most likely your organization has posted the grade or salary range internally. But one thing to keep in mind is that HR usually has policies around internal promotions and how much you can earn. Since the hiring manager often already knows how much you make, it's quite possible this question won't even be a factor. This allows you to focus on the benefits you can bring to the new opportunity. If you are an **external candidate**, this question leads us to the golden rule of negotiating during the job interview process: Postpone salary talk until the position has been offered to you! When asked about your salary expectations, ask what range they are working within. No matter what they say, it's always a good practice to respond, "I'll consider it." That gives you some time to go away and think about it without taking yourself out of the running.

Outside of tip #5, remember that your main goal in answering these questions is to get a second interview. Too many people psych themselves out because they think they have to get hired in their first meeting.

To further help people prepare for the many variations of the five types of interview questions, I've developed a deck of Interview Q & A Cards that will help you get prepared. I've had a number of clients who've used these, and they all agree that it gives them the confidence they need when going into an interview!

http://activ8careers.com/activ8-Q-and-A-playing-cards

The Ring In Action

THE RING OF INFLUENCE

Don't assume that just because you are an internal candidate you're a shoe-in over all the other external candidates. Get specific about your accomplishments and focus on what you can continue to bring the organization, not what's in it for you!

Action To Activ8

In the first section of this book you learned about and developed your branding statements, answering the value question. Now write out achievements that outline your skill sets so that you can call on them during an interview. Follow this formula and get specific!

WHAT YOU DID: (One sentence. This starts with an action word.)

_____

_____

HOW: _____

_____

_____

_____

RESULT: (One or two sentences.) _____

_____

_____

MANAGER'S
SPOTLIGHT

Acing the interview is just as important for the interviewer as it is the interviewee. Per a recent CareerBuilder survey of hiring managers about one bad hire:

▶ **24%** said it cost their business more than $50,000 in the last year.

▶ **40%** claimed it cost them more than $25,000 in the last year.

▶ **37%** lost money to recruit and train another worker.

▶ **38%** reported less productivity.

▶ **30%** stated the bad hire had a negative effect on employee morale.

▶ **21%** said it had a negative effect on client relations.

▶ **11%** reported fewer sales.

▶ **9%** experienced legal issues.

So the answer here is that just as someone going on an interview needs to ace the five kinds of questions, you need to ace reading potential hires in an interview. If you are interviewing someone for your team, develop very specific questions. Ask in a manner so that the interviewee is required to give real-life examples. This will show you how they think and work when put into situations similar to what they'll face in the role you're interviewing for. When they're answering, make sure you listen for a clear description of how they like to work and what unique value they will bring to your team. Listen for what they don't say as well – if they're not telling you what kind of unique value they'll deliver, they're probably not the right hire. In addition, when someone is late, interrupts you in the interview, or says something inappropriate, you can assume it's a sign of more to come. In summary, you get what you put into this process. The more prepared you are to conduct the interview, the more likely you are to hire the right person.

Here's a big watch-out when it comes to interviewing: Managers tend to hire people just like themselves. That's understandable (especially if you think you're good at your job!), however if you are not careful you might end up with a team or department that's not balanced. For example, if you already have a few people on your team (including yourself) who approach tasks with a Type A personality, you might want to consider other types, people who might balance out the pros and cons Type As bring to the team. I can personally testify about how valuable it is to team up with those who are different from me. They keep me in check, and as a team we often develop concepts and content that could only come from a team of different thinkers and skill sets.

So, my challenge to you is to hire someone smarter than yourself! One of the great mistakes we make as leaders is thinking that in order to be a great manager we have to know everything better than anyone else on the team. I've often said that the most successful employee is not the one who thinks they know everything, but rather the one who knows from whom to get the answers or resources. Hire candidates that are not satisfied with remaining in the status quo – ones who aren't just going to solve problems today, but be a force for your organization in the future.

The
ELEPHANT'S
unexpected
BATHROOM BREAK!

Strategy 8: Plan Ahead To Manage Unexpected Change

★ ★ ★ ★ ★ ★

How does the elephant trainer respond when an elephant pauses in the middle of a routine for a bathroom break? Or when a tightrope walker gets a foot injury and has to cope with missing a few performances? How we initially respond to adversity often decides whether or not we'll be successful in the face of change.

Up to this point in the book, we've been talking about how to manage change effectively and how you can create change for yourself. Now we'll transition to how you respond (or for some of you, *react*) when change strikes unexpectedly.

I'm sure you have you heard coworkers say that "S*#% Happens" when talking about change that just occurred. The following chart compares the percentages of people who create change, adopt change and even wait to accept change. Where would you say you fit in?

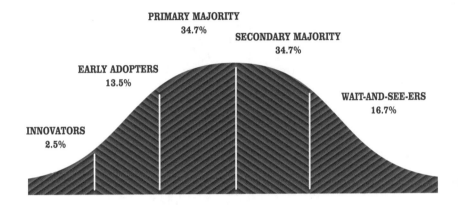

PRIMARY MAJORITY
34.7%

SECONDARY MAJORITY
34.7%

EARLY ADOPTERS
13.5%

WAIT-AND-SEE-ERS
16.7%

INNOVATORS
2.5%

This model was originally called the "Law of Diffusion of Innovation" – or in other terms, "change." It was created by Everett Rogers back in 1962 but is clearly still applicable today. The law explains how a new product is received in the market, breaking down the process into phases based on consumer types. This law is very commonly referred to in the marketing world, but I think it also applies to the phases of change acceptance.

The standard "Law of Diffusion of Innovation" bell curve is divided into five different segments with percentages that indicate how people respond to the new product. For us, the curve and segments can represent the different points at which individuals accept change.

As you can see on the curve, it's often easy to get the innovators and even some early adopters to accept the change. But the magic number is 16%. Research shows that if you can get 16% of your target audience to accept something new, you will have successfully crossed over to the point where a wave of acceptance of change occurs, resulting in real engagement.

In the following section, I've redefined this model with five change behaviors that mirror the behaviors featured in the "Law of Diffusion of Innovation" curve. Organizations who want to deliver change that engages their employees need to excel in identifying employees' change behaviors. Add to that effectively communicating change and addressing employees' concerns in order to ultimately experience what Malcom Gladwell has famously coined "the tipping point."

The Five "Acts" Of The Change Circus

There are several star performers in a circus, but the how and why behind their star quality is different. As I've said throughout this book, the way one engages change determines the potential to shine. When you read through the following circus-performer-as-behavior-profile analogies, ask yourself, "Which one of these descriptions best fits me?"

HOW THE CHANGE BEHAVIOR ASSESSMENT WORKS

As you know, purchasing this book entitles you to take the Change Behavior Assessment for free. The Behavior Assessment starts with 20 easy-to-answer questions about work and personal situations, measuring your reactions to various types of change. Your responses provide a map of your behaviors and attitudes against five possible star performer profiles. They are represented metaphorically by five performers in a classic circus: the Daredevil, Lion Tamer, Juggler, Tightrope Walker and Weight Lifter. Your personal assessment will identify how you are most likely to respond when you are asked (or forced) to make a change within your workplace.

WHAT IT MEASURES

These are the factors used to identify change behaviors:

1. COMFORT WITH RISK

How comfortable are you with personal and professional risk? How likely are you to embrace or avoid risk in day-to-day situations?

2. SPEED

How quickly do you make decisions when confronted with potential change?

3. LEAP OF FAITH

How much proof or evidence do you need to make a move versus being guided more by intuition?

4. REASSURANCE

How many people need to be on board before you will sign on to a new plan of action? Are you daring enough to be one of the first to commit to newer ways of doing things?

5. ADVENTUROUS SPIRIT

Does change in and of itself appeal to you because you are eager to try new things? In other words, even with no other compelling reason to support change, does the change itself attract you?

HOW ASSESSMENT RESULTS WILL HELP YOU ACHIEVE SUCCESS AT WORK

The self-awareness this profile provides can help you actively address change as it comes to you in your life and career. Once you have identified your natural tendencies, what's happening around you will become a great predictor of how you will respond to change in the future. The goal is to use this new level of awareness to not just let change happen, but to make changes work *for* you as they occur.

And while the assessment quiz is customized for each individual, it's built upon insights that are universal. For example, it's common to go through the day so focused on getting the job done that you fail to stop and recognize what's happening to you emotionally. We often respond in repeating patterns without thinking about our reactions. It's hard to overcome our less productive tendencies and respond to change rather than react to it. Most of us see change as an unwanted intruder. But when change hits, among other courses of action, we should take a long, hard look at our resistance to it and how to instead take steps toward a more constructive action plan. Knowing how to read the signs, including your own internal reactions to change, is critical if you ever want to master the art of making change work for you! And this assessment will help you identify those signs.

There's an old quote from iconic American educator Marva Collins that perfectly speaks to this topic: "Success doesn't come to you, you go to it." In other words, we can no longer just coast along, trying to maintain a status quo career. These days, most businesses are in constant flux. They must change, adapt, develop and progress if they are going to compete and survive. That means your career may continually change or evolve in order to fit into the future. The question to ask yourself is this: "Do I want to help *create* the change that's coming or just attempt to nail everything down?" Just look around. Most likely you'll see that change is happening, with or without you. Don't you want to be a part of making the change work *for* you? The self-awareness you achieve with this profile could be your first step to a healthier reaction to change.

HOW TO APPLY YOUR TEAM'S RESULTS AS THEIR MANAGER

Like it or not, most workers follow the direction of their managers. So the first step to helping your team deal positively with change is always looking at your own behaviors. Most people don't respect or follow managers who don't practice what they preach.

Using the results of the Profile Assessment, you can identify who you need to start having conversations with early. Who do you need to meet with so that they can speak about their concerns? More importantly, how do you develop a sound communication plan for your team, department or organization? Effective managers know their people and how to address their concerns. One size does not fit all!

In times of change, the goal as your team's manager should be to provide the right support in the right form at the right moment to help each of them as they process the changes happening. No two people respond to change in the same way. If you as a supervisor understand your team members' natural responses to change, you can direct their energy more quickly down a positive path to keep the team at its highest level of performance.

The Ring In Action

Learning how to redirect your thoughts around unexpected change is invaluable! Most of us react, never stopping to figure out how to manage our behaviors when change occurs. Trust me, those who learn how to favorably respond to unexpected change will have the upper hand in the long run. The faster you can check your emotions at the door and adapt to change the faster you will be able to focus on moving forward and creating a new approach to the change that will work for you. During these times of change you will separate yourself from the pack, developing a skill many others fail to ever recognize in their own careers.

When you redirect your emotions toward change, you will no longer be consumed with how any given change disrupts your life and career.

Let The Assessment Begin...

So, without further ado, it's time to introduce you to the five possible change profiles to which the Change Behavior Assessment will connect you. As you read through these introductions, you'll probably see parts of yourself in more than one profile – and that's a good thing! We're all unique individuals and no one is going to match 100% to one of these profiles. The Change Behavior Assessment takes that into account and will help you see which profile is your most dominant, followed by secondary profiles that also reflect part of who you are.

As you read through these, take a serious look at yourself.

Be honest in your strengths, weaknesses and opportunities.

And embrace how you're going to learn to manage change.

Profile #1
THE DAREDEVIL

★ ★ ★ ★ ★ ★

BACKGROUND

Whether it's the person who gets shot out of a cannon or the one who chooses to swing from the highest trapeze, the Daredevil is always ready to take a risk with little thought of the danger involved. Daredevils get a thrill from pushing themselves to higher levels of performance, achieving new and interesting feats. Even if there's risk involved, the thrill of doing something new is exciting, and this enthusiasm is contagious. The audience will no doubt be swept up in the Daredevil's daring performances.

THE DAREDEVIL PERSONALITY

Daredevils are high-energy people who need a place to express their ideas and concepts. When they have the right workplace environment (one that nurtures and focuses their energy), they can be unstoppable forces for growth, expansion and positive business evolution.

HOW DAREDEVILS DEAL WITH CHANGE

As stated earlier, when it comes to change in the workplace, Daredevils focus on the potential positive outcomes and rewards of the change rather than the potential risks involved. Their enthusiasm may even lead them to add new, personal ideas to the situation, pushing the change plan even faster or further.

Daredevils aren't afraid to share their vision or ideas when change happens. Even if it's not fully baked yet, Daredevils eagerly share their vision of the change with peers and coworkers. And because of their infectious enthusiasm, Daredevils can successfully implant their ideas in the minds of skeptical or hesitant team members.

However, Daredevils can be almost *too* willing to take a leap sometimes, getting caught up in their own enthusiasm to the point where they propose courses of action with unwarranted risk. After all, Daredevils tend to be dreamers. Sometimes their dreams come true. However, if they are not careful, the thrill of coming up with the idea often leads to them spending too much time dreaming of what *could* be rather than taking an action. Sometimes they fail. It's actually common for Daredevils to create or chase so many dreams that they cannot make them all a reality.

WHEN CONFRONTED WITH UNEXPECTED CHANGE, DAREDEVILS ARE LIKELY TO...

THINK: "These opportunities and possibilities are so exciting!"

SAY: "Can't wait to get started!"

DO: Take action.

The speed with which they process most changes: Almost immediate.

When faced with RISK, they will: Jump. Risk equals opportunity to Daredevils.

HOW MANAGERS CAN UTILIZE
AND ENCOURAGE DAREDEVILS

Harness and direct their abundant energy. Help them FOCUS their energy on a specific, constructive purpose.

Profile #2
THE LION TAMER

★ ★ ★ ★ ★ ★

BACKGROUND

Lion Tamers often find themselves center stage and having to figure out which lion to focus on. In this metaphor, the multiple lions a Lion Tamer has to manage represent the multiple changes that need attention within an organization at any given time. Effective Lion Tamers don't get distracted with all the changes roaring for their attention. They know focusing on a project and developing structure around the change is most effective. And while developing structure around acts of change, Lion Tamers can keep an eye out for what's happening around them. In other words, Lion Tamers are great at looking at the big picture, while also taking ownership of projects to meet the larger objective.

THE LION TAMER PERSONALITY

Lion Tamers are more comfortable being active. They get frustrated when there are no clear action steps for them to take. They hate standing around listening to the lions' roars of change!

HOW LION TAMERS DEAL WITH CHANGE

Lion Tamers deal best with change when they have a role in developing and controlling it. When asked to make a change happen, a Lion Tamer's first tendency is often to create a process or a framework. Denying them the freedom to create structure around the change will likely make them lose interest in being part of the team, and you can forget about them leading the charge around the change. The point is this: All Lion Tamers require is a small window of time in order to put some definition to the situation and build the structure that helps them begin.

To create an action plan, Lion Tamers want to understand the big, overriding objectives and goals. If they have these, they will tend to see the glass as half full and make the best of the situation, even if they are not completely sold on the need for change.

I'm sure you've noticed at the circus that Lion Tamers always use tools like whips or stools. They use these tools to develop and implement steps of action. The same thing goes in the workplace (minus the whips and stools, of course!). Workplace Lion Tamers are very strategic about which professional tools they use to manage change. This means that when asked to direct an act under pressure or in fearful circumstances, they're prepared to succeed.

WHEN CONFRONTED WITH UNEXPECTED CHANGE, LION TAMERS ARE LIKELY TO...

THINK: "I need to create a foundation and plan action steps."

SAY: "I have some questions about the big picture here... ."

DO: Plan and define.

The speed with which they process most changes: Quick.

When faced with RISK, they will: Need a moment to plan.

HOW MANAGERS CAN UTILIZE AND ENCOURAGE LION TAMERS

Explain the objectives and give them a project right away that will empower them to contribute toward these goals. If they are taking action, they feel more in control of the situation.

Profile #3
THE JUGGLER

★ ★ ★ ★ ★ ★

BACKGROUND

The talented Juggler is constantly evaluating where the next ball is falling, adjusting to catch it, then focusing on the next catch. With things flying at them all the time, a good Juggler knows that you need to be ready for the unexpected, and that the best plans can change quickly. Keeping the act flawless requires incredible attention to detail.

THE JUGGLER PERSONALITY

Jugglers are constantly weighing options and running "what if" scenarios through their heads. This helps them feel more prepared for the unknown. They spend a lot of time interpreting direction, looking for hidden meaning and trying to pin down what it means to them or their team.

HOW JUGGLERS DEAL WITH CHANGE

The Juggler tends to react to dramatic change with indecision. Why? Because the Juggler believes every change holds potential for being a good thing or a bad thing! Why? Because he's experienced both so often. He's seen great efforts lose their momentum unexpectedly, and vice versa. And so he reacts with a "wait and see" approach. Jugglers need some convincing that changes are necessary and that there's potential for great outcomes. So whether it's about new methods, processes, structure or any other proposed change, Jugglers are prone to proceed with some caution.

The Juggler sees his cautious, slow and steady approach as common sense and believes a careful course of action ultimately wins the race. A conservative speed allows him to adjust course and to weigh all his decisions carefully along the way.

WHEN CONFRONTED WITH UNEXPECTED CHANGE, JUGGLERS ARE LIKELY TO...

THINK: "I'm not totally convinced, but I'm open."

SAY: "I don't know. Maybe this change will be good. Maybe not."

DO: Ask others their opinions as part of the evaluation process.

The speed with which they process most changes: Moderate.

When faced with RISK, they will: Run mental "what if" scenarios to determine the worst and best possible personal outcomes related to the change.

HOW MANAGERS CAN UTILIZE AND ENCOURAGE JUGGLERS

If you're a manager, give the Jugglers on your team some time. In fact, if possible, it's helpful to communicate to Jugglers before the change is upon them. Giving them some warning helps them process things on their own terms. Talk through the situation with them, focusing on logical points and rational justifications for the change.

Profile #4
THE TIGHTROPE WALKER

★ ★ ★ ★ ★ ★

BACKGROUND

The circus Tightrope Walker defies danger and death itself, walking carefully on a thin wire from one side of the tent to the other. Even with the added burden of props – sometimes even other high-wire artists on his back! – a talented Tightrope Walker knows that a very slow and cautious speed is the key. Close attention to every detail diminishes the likelihood of disaster.

THE TIGHTROPE WALKER PERSONALITY

Tightrope Walkers are skeptics by nature. They've had to find balance on some very thin lines over the years, and desire hard facts to support any kind of change to what already works. They must firmly plant each step before considering the next.

HOW THE TIGHTROPE WALKER DEALS WITH CHANGE

For the Tightrope Walker, the devil is always in the details!

These individuals will move toward change *only* if they thoroughly understand all the implications of it. Tightrope Walkers will always prefer rolling out a complex plan in stages so that it can be checked along the way.

They always ask why a change is happening and insist on straight answers. They won't be swayed by a supervisor's expression of hope or inspiration. Even the blind faith of coworkers will not be persuasive. Facts and details are what work for the Tightrope Walker.

Knowing that, it shouldn't be a surprise that Tightrope Walkers resist change that is happening fast. They may even take steps to slow things down so they have time to define and digest the details of the situation. This sometimes manifests in their being divisive in a team setting, especially if they do not have all the details, much less the time they want to mentally process the proposed changes. If not given both, they will often challenge the situation *and* the people bringing rapid change into their lives.

WHEN CONFRONTED WITH UNEXPECTED CHANGE, TIGHTROPE WALKERS ARE LIKELY TO...

THINK: "I'm really skeptical this change is right."

SAY: "Why is this change so important? I need more details about why this is happening."

DO: Gather information.

The speed with which they process most changes: Slow.

When faced with RISK, they will: Gather facts to control the situation and then "test" the convictions and logic of the person driving the change.

HOW MANAGERS CAN UTILIZE AND ENCOURAGE TIGHTROPE WALKERS

You have to give Tightrope Walkers every bit of information and detail that you can. Details equal empowerment for this personality. And as was the case with the Juggler, give them time to process before expecting action. In doing so, you'll create a "safety net" of detail and time under the Tightrope Walker, getting them to venture one step at a time. By creating the net, you've provided assurance, allowing them to rethink any step that doesn't work out as planned, and thereby minimizing their risk.

Profile #5
THE WEIGHT LIFTER

★ ★ ★ ★ ★ ★

BACKGROUND

One of the most classic characters in a circus is the Weight Lifter, amazing audiences by lifting heavier amounts than most can even imagine. Barbells that look as if they weigh more than a car are hoisted overhead to the applause of people who didn't believe lifting them was possible.

THE WEIGHT LIFTER PERSONALITY

The Weight Lifter's joy comes from astounding audiences with feats he's done thousands of times. When it comes to the workplace, Weight Lifters have often been in the organization, or at least in the industry, for a long time. They have likely carved out unique niches in the company by being the only one who can perform a particular kind of task, or who has a unique expertise in a certain area. For this reason, they usually feel pretty safe in their roles and believe they are hard to replace. Managers tend to heap great praise on their Weight Lifter team members, considering them the backbone of the team.

HOW WEIGHT LIFTERS DEAL WITH CHANGE

Weight Lifters are the most likely to be strongly attached to the way things have been done before. After all, they've thrived doing it "the old way." Thus, they resist most types of change. However, they do respond better to change if they are first given a chance to voice their concerns. They must be heard if they are to ever move on!

Let's take a step back. At the first sight of change, Weight Lifters may not care to be included, and may actually rather be left alone. They see current methods and roles as their safety blanket, wondering why anyone would change things – even if the proposed changes might improve things. Some Weight Lifters use phrases like, "I'm too old to change." They love the phrase, "If it ain't broke, don't fix it."

Managers are advised to listen to the Weight Lifter though. They have the history and knowledge to help improve a plan for change, and if you can get them on your side they will be a major force for change. If you include them in the decision-making process, they are likely to quickly get on board.

WHEN CONFRONTED WITH UNEXPECTED CHANGE, WEIGHT LIFTERS ARE LIKELY TO...

THINK: "Oh no. This is not necessary. Things are fine the way they are."

SAY: "This is a mistake." However, they may not say it out loud unless they know others think the same way.

DO: Bare minimum asked. Mostly they'll try to lay low and avoid attention. They may be building their case for fighting the changes.

The speed with which they process most changes: Almost zero.

When faced with RISK, they will: Exhibit one of two very different reactions:

1. Go through the motions and play along, but show discontent through body language and tone of voice.

2. Recruit others around the idea that the new change is bad, building power in numbers.

HOW MANAGERS CAN UTILIZE AND ENCOURAGE WEIGHT LIFTERS

Ask them questions and get them talking about their fears around the change. Helping them voice their concerns will begin the process of helping them accept the change. This is where the TQM (Total Quality Management) concept comes into play. A common approach in the business world, TQM is founded upon the idea that the quality of products and processes is the responsibility of every person within an organization who is involved with either the development and/or distribution of a product or service. TQM was developed several decades ago to help multiple employee "types" become more integrated, and it definitely helps Weight Lifters get on board. This practice allows and empowers workers to figure out how to implement change and new processes. Today we have advanced the TQM concept into what is known as Six Sigma, a more complex combination of quality management methods. But regardless of whether it's TQM or Six Sigma, the idea, in short, is to get Weight Lifters involved in the process as soon as possible!

The
GRAND FINALE

AND THAT,
LADIES AND GENTLEMEN,
IS OUR SHOW!

★ ★ ★ ★ ★ ★

As "change" enters the room every day, every week of every year, the question is: Will you manage it? Embrace it? Transform it? Or will you just let change define you without interacting with it?

Ringmasters Know The Following:

1. THEIR ROLE

They perform within their defined strengths and personal brand. They are confident, not arrogant. They see opportunities and clearly take on what's within their ability to control. They make things happen.

2. HOW AND WHEN TO GET INVOLVED

They look for ways to create agreements, lead others to come to solutions, or compel others to follow their great example.

3. WHO'S DIRECTING CHANGE

They know how to respond rather than react to delegated change.

The goal of every organization is to create growth, and that means there will be constant change. I often hear employees or job seekers say the same thing: "I just want a job that is secure. One that I know won't be taken from me. One where I will always be needed." They want promises and guarantees that don't exist.

But knowing how to manage the three rings of change and finding confidence in yourself will equip and empower your career and life.

You will be at peace with yourself, knowing that whatever happens, you are the Ringmaster.

You can manage what comes your way.

So put on your top hat and become the Ringmaster you were meant to be!

Manager's Spotlight: References For Statistics

THE THREE RINGS OF CHANGE

1. http://www.thesocialworkplace.com/2011/08/08/social-knows-employee-engagement-statistics-august-2011-edition/

THE SECRET FOUND IN STAR PERFORMERS

1. "Why, How & What" - Simon Sinek

2. http://blog.seattlepi.com/workplacewrangler/2010/03/05/do-you-know-your-employees-strengths/

ATTENTION, LADIES AND GENTLEMEN

1. Kinni, Theodore. "Loosen up your communication style." Harvard Business School *Working Knowledge* newsletter, 30 June 2003. Retrieved from http://hbswk.hbs.edu/tools/print_item.jhtml?id=3559&t=organizations.

2. Melcrum Research. "Making managers better communicators: tools and techniques for best-practice line manager communication." Melcrum Publishing Ltd, 2004, http://www.melcrum.com.

3. *Excel with employee communication – the core area of PR practice*, by Kim Harrison, which you can access at www.cuttingedgepr.com

DON'T HIDE FROM THE SPOTLIGHT

1. http://www.zeromillion.com/business/personnel/employee-productivity.html

WARNING: PERFORMANCES MAY VARY

1. http://www.corporateculturepros.com/2010/08/corporate-culture-madness-leaders-pay-attention/

2. http://www.thesocialworkplace.com/2011/08/08/social-knows-employee-engagement-statistics-august-2011-edition/

PLANNING FOR YOUR STARDOM INTO THE FUTURE

1. http://guides.wsj.com/management/strategy/how-to-set-goals/

THE BIG-TOP DOESN'T RAISE ITSELF

1. http://www.connectionsonline.net/news/strategy-execution.aspx

THE AUDITIONS COUNT

1. http://www.careerbuilder.com/share/aboutus/pressreleasesdetail.aspx?id=pr609&sd=12/13/2010&ed=12/31/2010

THE ELEPHANT'S UNEXPECTED BATHROOM BREAK

1. http://en.wikipedia.org/wiki/Diffusion_of_innovations

2. http://innovateordie.com.au/2010/05/10/the-secret-to-accelerating-diffusion-of-innovation-the-16-rule-explained/

Other Books
by David W. Hults

From Cornered To Corner Office (Overcoming Career Obstacles)

From Roadkill To Roadmap (Career Search Campaign)

From Fish Story To Success Story (Effective Networking)

From Desperation To Deal (Negotiating The Job Offer)

Acknowledgements

Brad Fuller is my amazing partner who understands and encourages me to live a full life. Because of Brad, I've achieved more than I ever thought I could. Thank you for being my best friend, trusted advocate and an expert advisor. Because of your support, I'm better able to provide value and personal growth for all who experience Activ:8 Careers.

Thanks to my right hand man, Travis Ulmer, who generously provides me with expertise as an editor and sought out social media expert. I couldn't have done it without you!

Special thanks to my professional business coach, Lois Creamer, whose "Book More Business" approach has helped me envision what *could* be. You continually encouraged me to make this book happen, and thus, *Ringmaster* was born.